My Mummy is Autistic

A Picture Book and Guide about Recognising and Understanding Difference

Heath Grace
Joanna Grace

 Routledge
Taylor & Francis Group

LONDON AND NEW YORK

First published 2021
by Routledge
2 Park Square, Milton Park, Abingdon, Oxon OX14 4RN

and by Routledge
52 Vanderbilt Avenue, New York, NY 10017

Routledge is an imprint of the Taylor & Francis Group, an informa business

British Library Cataloguing-in-Publication Data
A catalogue record for this book is available from the British Library

Library of Congress Cataloging-in-Publication Data
Names: Grace, Heath, author. | Grace, Joanna, author.
Title: My mummy is autistic: a picture book and guide about recognising and understanding difference / Heath Grace, Joanna Grace.
Description: Abingdon, Oxon ; New York, NY : Routledge, [2020]
Identifiers: LCCN 2020007704 (print) | LCCN 2020007705 (ebook) |
ISBN 9780367510633 (hardback) | ISBN 9780367460235 (paperback) |
ISBN 9781003026518 (ebook) Subjects: LCSH: Grace, Joanna–Mental health. |
Autism–Juvenile literature. Classification: LCC RC553.A88 G72 2020 (print) |
LCC RC553.A88 (ebook) | DDC 616.85/882–dc23
LC record available at https://lccn.loc.gov/2020007704
LC ebook record available at https://lccn.loc.gov/2020007705

ISBN: 978-0-367-51063-3 (hbk)
ISBN: 978-0-367-46023-5 (pbk)
ISBN: 978-1-003-02651-8 (ebk)

Typeset in DIN
by Newgen Publishing UK

To Tigger for always being our friend, however we communicated

Contents

Foreword

Articulating what is like to be autistic is unfortunately almost impossible as a child or young adult. For a start there is a lack of vocabulary and an inability to comprehend context, but more fundamentally we can't actually understand that we are different, we cannot see or place ourselves in the broader world – because we don't yet relate to that world. To that extent we are incapacitated and vulnerable. That vulnerability is dangerous, because as we mature it is exposed and our differences lead to increasing degrees of separation, a normally painful process.

As adults, who have worked through these difficulties and 'survived', we can begin to grapple with our abilities and inabilities, and when we find the courage we can explain these to others and begin to modify our world to better allow us to co-habit and interact with others. But that is a very definitely adult asset.

What is unique about this book is that it translates the brutal truth of a child's observations of an adult into the 'grown-up' reality of someone who is conscious of their autism and all the consequences it entails. Being a parent is always painful – everyone makes mistakes, but here the parent is grappling with differences which may be difficult for the child to understand. And yet there is a remarkable tenderness here, between mother and child, an acceptance which is both beautiful and charming and heart-warming. The drawings offer a clarity, the voice of the child a purity, uncomplicated and direct. But of course what seals its success is the equally honest and pragmatic replies from the adult.

It is only with this forthright and clear expression of an autistic reality that others can ever be aware of the differences. We share the same times and spaces in the same world, but we don't sense or feel it in the same way. We have attributes and difficulties, but that world needs us, because sometimes our minds have solutions which others can't see or imagine. We don't think 'outside the box' . . . because for us there is no box.

And there is no box for autistic people either, it's a spectrum condition, we are all different at being different. So my perspective will be similar, but not the same as other people with a diagnosis of autism. All I, we, can ask is for people to accept and understand us. We don't want to be tolerated, partitioned, pitied or marginalised. We can integrate and succeed, we can be good parents, raise good children, smart children, kind children . . . we will just need to do it in a slightly different way.

Chris Packham, Broadcaster, Environmentalist and Author

My Mummy is Autistic.

My Mummy is autistic.

Our brains work differently.

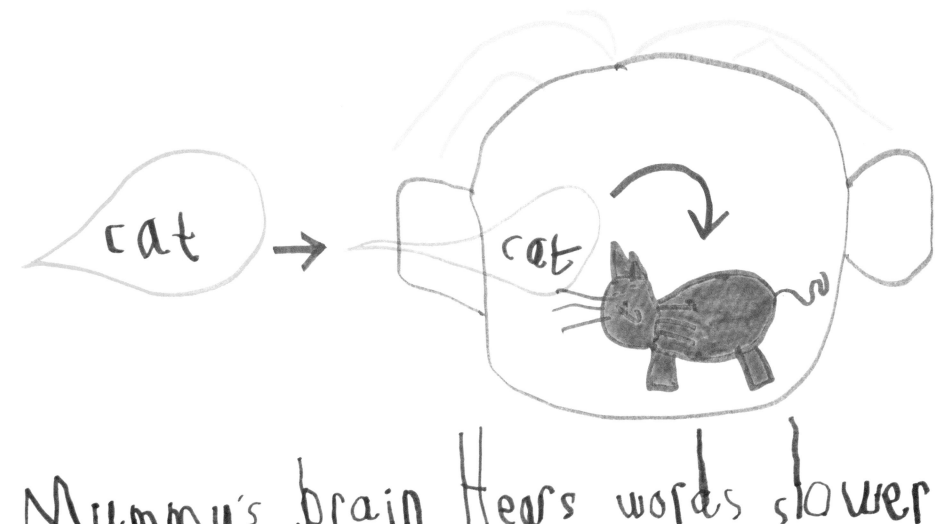

Mummy's brain Hears words slower than my brain. My brain hears words quickly.

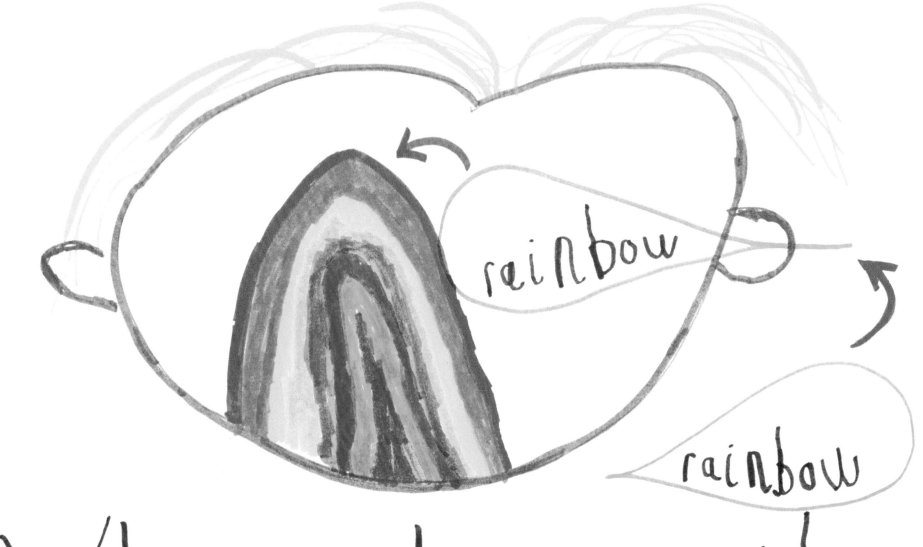

When a word comes into my brain I know what it means right away!

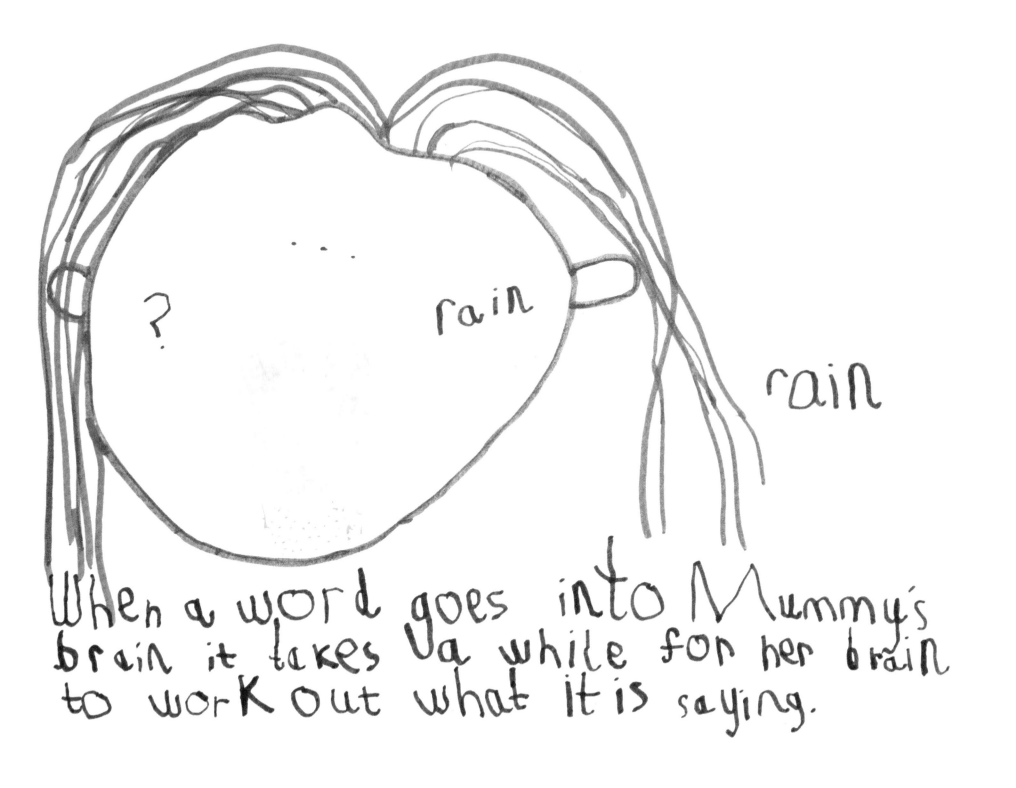

?   rain

rain

When a word goes into Mummy's brain it takes a while for her brain to work out what it is saying.

If I say lots of words they get stuck in a queue in mummy's brain and I have a long wait until she hears me.

If I say one or two words I only have a little wait until she hears me.

I always say "MUMMY" so she knows
I am talking to her.

Sometimes the words waiting in Mummy's head get muddled up and she hears them in the wrong order!

Take off your clothes and get in the water.

Hearing words in the wrong order can be very funny.

Sometimes the words Mummy says get muddled and she stops talking in the middle of a sentence. I remind her to keep on talking.

Abaracadaba?

Pass the crisps.

What is the magic words?

We both forget to say "please" sometimes.
I am getting better at remembering.
I remind Mummy.

This is my listening face

This is My Mummy's listening face.

This is me talking to my
friend.

This is Mummy talking to her friend.

The other Mummies and daddies like to chat when they are waiting for us to come out of school.

My Mummy likes to play.

I like to play with my Mummy

My Mummy has lots of ideas. Her brain is good at thinking.

I love my Mummy.

NOTES FROM MUMMY

Mummy is autistic

My Mummy is autistic.

Like many autistic women of my age, I was diagnosed in adulthood. The world is rich with deficit narratives about autism. Even though my conscious mind knows it is a different brain not a broken brain, my subconscious is still littered with the same prejudices everyone else's is. Getting diagnosed did not change who I am; the diagnosis did not give me autism, I was autistic all along. But it did make me more aware of my own subjectivity and fallibility. Getting diagnosed led me to question the effect of my autism on my parenting. Would my young son suffer in some way because his Mummy was autistic? Does being different do harm?

Like all parents, sometimes I am brilliant and sometimes I am dreadful. My autism is all of me, I could no more point to a part of me that is not autistic than could a neurotypical person point to a part of themselves that is not neurotypical. Autism has contributed to some superb parenting and some awful parenting. Being different does not do harm. What I have noticed through my journey with my son is that when harm is caused it is often due to a lack of understanding of difference, rather than the difference itself.

The book you have in your hands came about one summer when my son and I quite literally bumped into a difference in understanding in the supermarket. He was riding on the front of the shopping trolley, in charge of the shopping list and looking out for the items we were to buy. We work as a team when we shop. We have an established system: if he sees an item, he tells me to stop the trolley and then he hops off to get it. If I see an item, I stop the trolley and point it out to him so that he can fetch it. If it is on a high shelf, I get it. Usually, we work with few words and a great deal of focus.

But on this occasion he had a lot to say. I was listening to his excited monologue as we manoeuvred through the aisles. I was struggling to keep up with the flow of what he was telling me. Midway through a sentence he spotted an item from our list, said "stop" and got off the trolley. I did not hear the "stop" as swiftly as I would usually have done because I was still trying to figure out the earlier part of his sentence. Consequently I did not stop the trolley in time. It bumped into his ankles and he was hurt. Not seriously hurt, but both his body and his heart were sore. He stood in the aisle looking up at me and said in wounded tones "But I said stop Mummy?"

I felt very sorry. I had let him down. I had hurt his little body and his big feelings. I apologised and we continued with the shopping. Outside the supermarket I realised that my committing to never make the same "mistake" again would not work. I am very liable to do the same thing in the same circumstances, because my "mistake" was not a lack of paying attention or a lack of effort. Trying harder will not make me any less autistic. He had had my whole concentration. My "mistake" was a facet of the brain I have. I owed him an explanation.

I explained the situation that had happened in the supermarket to him and, although he had only just turned five at the time, he seemed to understand. At breakfast the following morning I asked him to explain it to me to see if he had absorbed what I had said. He drew a picture as he talked. His explanation was crystal clear. I told him that his explanation was so good I thought he might be able to explain it to other people. The long summer holidays were approaching and so he set to the task of writing this book for you. It was no small undertaking for him. The words in it are all his own. I have helped him with the order in places, and suggested that he think of a beginning and an ending, but in general I was just an assistant, the work in the book is his. He has explained the difference we bumped into in the supermarket and in doing so he touches on some other differences that I exhibit that I may have in common with other autistic people. We very much hope this book helps you to understand better the differences you might bump into, in supermarkets and in the wider world.

Our brains work differently

Our brains work differently.

One of my favourite analogies for being autistic is to imagine our brains are computers. We all know that there are different types of computers. One type of computer may be better at a particular task than another type of computer. Being better at that task does not mean that it is a better computer, only that it is good at that task. If we asked it to do a different job it might be worse at it than the other type of computer. When I was growing up I had a BBC Micro computer to play computer games on and my friend had a ZX Spectrum. If I tried to play one of my friend's games on my computer it would not work. That didn't mean my computer was broken, just that I was trying to get it to do the wrong sort of thing. Likewise, if my friend tried to play one of my computer games on their computer it would not have worked either.

Imagine your brain is a computer. Being autistic means you have a different type of brain to people who are neurotypical. All of our brains have things they are good at and things they are bad at. Your brain might seem broken if you ask it to do things it is not wired to do. But if you ask it to do things it is wired to do then it will seem brilliant.

Scientists are still learning about the brain, there may be many more types of brain to be discovered. Think about what your brain is good at. Whatever type of brain you have it will be bad at some things and brilliant at others.

Mummy's brain hears words slower than my brain. My brain hears words quickly

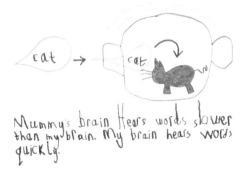

Mummy's brain hears words slower than my brain. My brain hears words quickly.

You can think of understanding language as a two-step process.

First of all, if you are listening to someone talking your ears have to hear what they are saying. If you cannot hear them clearly you will not be able to understand what they are saying.

You might be reading someone's writing or sign language, in which case the first step for you would be for your eyes to see what was being said. If your eyes cannot see clearly then you will not be able to understand what is being said.

The second step to understanding language is for your brain to take what your senses have told it and work out what that means. Your senses might tell your brain that they have heard or seen the word "cat"; your brain has to then work out that that word means a four-legged animal with pointy ears and fur, that says "meow". Once your brain has worked out what the word means, you have understood what was said.

If your ears hear the word "cat" but your brain does not know what it means, you do not understand what is being said. Imagine hearing someone speaking a language you do not know. You can do the first step of understanding perfectly: your senses tell you what word was said, but you cannot do the second step so you do not understand.

When a word comes into my brain I know what it means right away!

When a word goes into Mummy's brain it takes a while for her brain to work out what it is saying

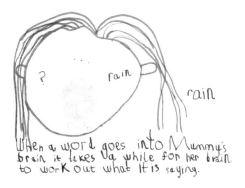

Autistic brains have been shown to understand language slower than neurotypical brains. We do not know why this is. Some people think the parts of autistic brains that do the working out work more slowly than the parts of the neurotypical brains that do the working out. Other people think that autistic brains want to understand each word more thoroughly than neurotypical brains, so they spend longer on each word to check they have understood it sufficiently.

If I say lots of words they get stuck in a queue in Mummy's brain and I have a long wait until she hears me

If I say lots of words they get stuck in a queue in mummy's brain and I have a long wait until she hears me.

If I say one or two words I only have a little wait until she hears me

If I say one or two words I only have a little wait until she hears me.

Sometimes the words waiting in Mummy's head get muddled up and she hears them in the wrong order!

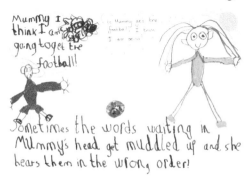

Sometimes the words waiting in Mummy's head get muddled up and she hears them in the wrong order!

Hearing words in the wrong order can be very funny

Not understanding is not the same as not hearing. When my little boy talks to me I listen to him and I hear every word. But when he says a lot of words I do not understand them all as quickly as he says them.

Have you ever watched fireworks from a long way away? If you have you know that you see the light of the fireworks exploding a few moments before you hear the "bang" from that explosion. It is the same with thunder and lightning, as a thunder storm approaches you see the lightning flash seconds before you hear the thunder roll. If you could watch what is going on inside my head you would experience a similar wait. You would spot me hearing the words and then a few moments later you would spot me understanding the words.

Autism is a spectrum. This means it is different for everyone with autism. Neurotypicism is a spectrum. Everyone who is neurotypical is different. There is no one way of being autistic, any more than there is one way of being neurotypical. For me, the distance between hearing and understanding is a matter of seconds, for other autistic people it could be much quicker or much slower. The same is true for neurotypical people, some will understand language quicker than others. Everyone is different. All we know is that most autistic people understand language slower than most neurotypical people.

When someone speaks to me I hear their words at the same speed as they say them, but I do not understand them at that speed. So all the words go in, they are all heard, but it takes a while for the part of my brain that works out what they mean to understand them. My son thinks of this as being like the words waiting in a line in my head to take their turn in the part of the brain that works out what they mean. Like anything lining up they can get bored and fidget around. If words get understood in the wrong order it can change the meaning of what is being said.

Consider the instruction to "Take off your clothes and jump in the water"; heard in the right order this instruction asks you to get undressed and then get into the water. But if those words got jumbled up in your understanding you could hear "Take off your clothes and jump in the water" but understand it as "jump in the water and take off your clothes" which would result in you getting your clothes rather soggy!

It is useful when giving instructions to consider whether they would mean the same in another order. Or to give them in small chunks so that they cannot get muddled. So for the example above you might say to someone "Take off your clothes" and then wait until they had done that before saying "jump in the water".

I always say "Mummy" so she knows I am talking to her

i always say "MUMMy" so she knows
I am talking to her

There is a lot of language around in the world. People who can understand language quickly may choose to listen in on the language around them because they are curious. People who understand language slowly may choose not to listen in, because if they listened all the time they would get very tired.

Imagine a busy room with lots of people talking. If you are listening in a little bit on all the conversations and the person in front of you says "Would you like a cup of tea?", you probably know that they are talking to you. If you are not listening in on all the conversations you will not hear the person saying "Would you like a cup of tea?" even though they are standing right in front of you.

Think about being those people.

The person standing in the busy room who has a brain that can listen in on all the conversation hears the offer of a cup of tea and can have one if they want it. They can also enjoy eavesdropping on what is being said around them.

The person standing in the busy room who has a brain that cannot listen in on all the conversations does not hear the offer of the cup of tea so does not get to have one even if they want one. They cannot listen to what everyone is saying and so might feel quite left out even though there are lots of people around them.

The person offering the cup of tea to the person who can listen gets an answer to their question.

The person offering the cup of tea to the person who cannot listen does not get an answer to their question. If they do not understand that some brains are different they might feel upset for being ignored and they might also think the other person is being rude. If they do understand that some brains are different they will not feel upset and might try to find another way to offer the other person a cup of tea.

A good tip is to always start what you are saying with a person's name, this can help people to know that the words you say next are for them.

Sometimes the words Mummy says get muddled and she stops talking in the middle of a sentence. I remind her to keep talking

When I am talking I have to use the part of my brain that works out what words mean, this is the part of my brain that works more slowly than the same part in a neurotypical brain. Instead of asking it what a word means, I am giving it a meaning and asking what word I need to use to describe that meaning.

If it is something I have said before and my brain has had practice at finding the words, I am usually pretty good at this part. We are all often better at outputting language than inputting it. This means we are better at speaking than at listening, or better at explaining what we mean through our writing than we are at understanding what someone else means by reading their writing.

If I am trying to describe something new to me or something that feels very important or very emotional my brain can get stuck finding the words I need. Sometimes my brain gets stuck finding the words because it is thinking about other things at the same time. A lot of autistic people care a great deal about getting things right, and making the extra effort to ensure we say things to the best of our abilities can take a bit of time. A lot of autistic people have had experiences of saying something in the wrong way when their brain didn't work out the right thing to say and they do not want to do this again, so they have extra worries to contend with when trying to find the words to say.

I plan the sentences I say lots of times in my head before I say them out loud. This is because I want to get them right. When I say them out loud they sound just the same as they sounded in my head. Sometimes I stop talking because I think I have already said the thing I am saying. Sometimes I have, but other times I have only said it inside my head, and not outside my head to the person I am talking to. This means the person listening to me hears the start of my sentence and then all of a sudden in the middle of the sentence I stop talking.

When my son tells me I have stopped talking this is really useful to me because I do not know that I stopped in the wrong place. When he tells me it is easy for me to finish saying the sentence that I had planned to say. Sometimes I think I have said something out loud when I actually said all of it inside my head, this is much more confusing for everyone!

We both forget to say "please" sometimes. I am getting better at remembering. I remind Mummy

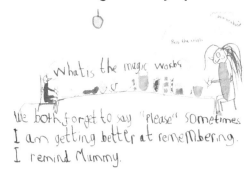

Some of the things we say are useful and some of the things we say are to make our language kind. For example when I say "Give me the bread" this is useful, you know I want you to pass me the bread. When I say "Please give me the bread" this hasn't got any extra usefulness to it, but it has got a bit of kindness. The word "please" lets you know that I am not just bossing you around, it is a way of being nice to you as a person.

When someone has to work very hard to work out the useful bits of language they are less likely to remember the kind parts of language. Everyone is prone to forgetting the kind parts of language when they are tired.

Think about two examples.

The first person is selfish, they think other people should do all their work for them, when they ask for bread they expect to be given it just because they have asked. They say "Give me the bread"; they are being rude.

The second person finds it difficult to find the right words to ask the question they want to ask. They care about what you think of their words and want to get them right. They work so hard on getting it right that their brain gets tired and forgets the kind parts of the sentence. They say "Give me the bread"; they sound rude.

You can understand that even though both of these people say something that sounds rude there is a difference between how they felt about the person they were talking to. When we understand the differences between people it can help us not to feel offended when no offence was meant.

We should all use the kind words as well as the useful words, regardless of our differences. I do not teach my son that I do not have to use the kind words because I am autistic. I teach my son that he should help people to remember the kind words. As he has grown up, lots of people have helped him to remember these words, his teachers, friends, family, and even me. He is happy to help other people remember the kind words and understands that some people might always need help to remember.

This is my listening face

This is my listening face

This is my Mummy's listening face

This is My Mummy's listening face.

This is me talking to my friend

This is me talking to my friend.

This is Mummy talking to her friend

This is Mummy talking to her friend.

Many autistic people do not look to make eye contact when in conversation with someone. This can be very hard for neurotypical people to understand. Neurotypical people like to look at each other's faces and into each other's eyes when they talk.

When I talk to people I naturally turn myself so that I am positioned as Heath has drawn me in the picture: at a 45-degree angle from the person. Over the course of my life I have had many people tell me to "Look at me when I am talking to you" or "show me that you are listening by looking at me". In general I have a choice. I can look at you, or I can listen to you. If you want me to listen to you, why do you ask me to look? It seems very strange to me, you say you want me to use my ears, to listen, but then you tell me to use my eyes, to look.

I am in my forties, so I have learned over time how to work around neurotypicals' need for me to look at them when I am listening to them. I look at the air next to someone's head, or I look at their shoulder. Sometimes I try to look at their nose. I wonder … do you really want me looking at your nose when you talk? Maybe you would like it more if I listened to you talk but did not look at you?

I have to concentrate to remember to look at the air near your head, or your shoulder. If what you are saying is really interesting it is likely that it will fill my concentration so I will not have any left over for remembering to look at your nose, or look near your face and will stop looking at you. If you believe I have a neurotypical brain you will probably understand my looking away to indicate that I have gotten bored with what you are saying. But if you understand that I have an autistic brain then you will understand that my looking away shows that I am giving what you are saying all of my concentration.

Certain situations are easier for me to talk and listen in than others. For example I do very well having conversations with people in cars, especially if I am driving. If I am driving no one expects me to look at them. I can happily talk for hours to my passenger and listen to them. Walking side by side works too. But the easiest way for me to talk to someone is via video chat. Why?

Well, when I am talking to you in real life I know there are lots and lots of other things you want me to be doing: you want me to be looking at you, you want me to make facial expressions that match what I am saying and also to make facial expressions to match what you are saying. Neurotypical people do all of these things without having to think about them, but I have to concentrate on doing them all. To concentrate on making facial expressions I not only have to make the expressions I also have to think about whether I am making them, and whether they are the right ones. It is as if I have to keep watch on my own face and report back to my brain about whether it is doing what it is supposed to be doing, and then my brain sends a message to tell my face what to do. There are two jobs: the reporting job, and the message-sending job.

Imagine if I said, when you talk to me I want you to juggle at the same time and as well as juggling I want you to write letters backwards in the air in front of us. Juggling would take a lot of your concentration (that is me being told to look at you) and writing the letters would mean you would need to think about what the letters should look like, and then turn them over and write them backwards (so it is two jobs, like the reporting and messaging I need to do in order to make facial expressions). It would be a lot to ask! And actually if you did none of it at all I would still be able to hear your words and understand what you are saying.

If I can see a video I do not look at the other person, I look at me. The other person does not know that I am looking at me, because we are both on screen and the camera points out at me as I look, it looks to them as if I am looking (so that is one less job). When I can see myself on screen I do not need to wonder in my head if I am making facial expressions, I can just see it, so I no longer need to do the reporting job. I am actually down to just one job: remembering to make facial expressions. Compared to the three jobs of looking, reporting and messaging I have to do when we talk in real life, it is much much easier!

People find it hard to understand why making eye contact is difficult for autistics. I do too. Some people say because autistic brains take in so much information that the additional information of a face with all its expressions is overwhelming. That could be it. From my own experience of making eye contact when talking, the best analogy I can draw for it is like having pins and needles. It feels very intense and if you move it gets worse and you just want to get away.

I find it hard to understand why it matters so much. With cats and dogs we are quite happy to understand that a dog wagging its tail means it is happy, where as a cat wagging its tail means it is cross. We do not try to change the response of either, we simply understand the difference. If people understood that some people listen by looking and listening and some people listen by thinking and listening then we could just get on with being ourselves. Heath is only five but to him it is common sense, Mummy listens this way, I listen that way. It is not complicated to him, why should it be for anyone else?

The other Mummies and Daddies like to chat when they are waiting for us to come out of school

My Mummy likes to play

People are sociable creatures. Have you ever seen a group of chimpanzees grooming each other, picking small bits of dirt out of one another's fur? Did you know they do that to each other even when they are clean? It is their way of saying "I will look after you, I care for you".

Humans use something called "small talk" in the same way that chimpanzees use grooming. By saying little things to each other they let one another know that they care for them and are interested in their wellbeing. People might talk about the weather or share little bits of information about their day.

To people who understand language quickly, small talk is enjoyable. It is a comfortable way to spend time in each other's company. For people whose brains do not understand language quickly and who want to be sure to get what they say right, small talk can be tiring and confusing. Tiring because there is so much of it and it is not clear what it is about (that's because it is not really about anything), and confusing because they want to get it right (and there isn't really a "right" thing to say, although there are – as I have found – lots of ways to get it wrong!)

As I have to think so hard about my words I like to make sure I am thinking about things I think are important, so that the worth of what I say matches the effort I have to put into saying it. This means I am not very good at small talk, but surprisingly I am quite good at giving speeches.

Like a lot of autistic people my age, I remember the school playground as being a scary place. When I went to school people did not understand difference in the way that they do now. I did not do or say the same things as the other children and lots of misunderstandings happened. The other children thought I did not want to play, they thought I was rude or stuck up, they thought I was odd. It was hard for me to understand them and hard for them to understand me.

My son started school last year, and for the first time in a long time I had to stand in a playground again. It made me feel very uncomfortable. It reminded me of a lot of sad times. At first I tried to join in with the small talk. I have practiced my small talk a lot since I was at school. I get better at it the older I get and the more I understand it, but I am still noticeably bad at it if you compare me to people my age with neurotypical brains who are so good at it and seem to be able to do it without even trying.

After a while of trying to join in with the small talk and not really managing I decided to stop trying. I enjoy standing next to people and not talking. I hope the grown-ups in the playground do not misunderstand my not joining in with their small talk in the same way that the children in the playground used to misunderstand me when I was younger. I like to think we all share that space together and that we are all showing in our own way our concern and care for one another.

I like to play with my Mummy

I like to play with my Mummy

I have begun to play whilst the other grown-ups are chatting. I am learning to hula hoop and I like to practice a lot. Autistic brains are often very good at focusing on things. Neurotypical brains tend not to be so good at focusing, sometimes they find the focus of an autistic mind worrying. When I hula hoop whilst the other grown-ups are chatting I feel really happy. It has taken me a long time to find a way of being me with other people. Growing up I thought I was supposed to fix my differences. Now I realise I just have to understand them and help other people to understand them too.

A great way to play with me is to join in with an activity that I love. My son is learning to hula hoop too and when we hoop together we both have fun playing and being with one another. If you know someone who is autistic and is interested in a particular activity or topic and you want to share time with them, try showing an interest in their interest. If you are autistic and you have a particular activity or topic you are interested in and you want to share time with someone who is neurotypical, try thinking about which parts of your interest they might also be interested in and share these with them.

I have spent a lot of time thinking about the ways in which I am different and wondering if they make me better or worse than the next person. I have worried that my differences will hurt me or hurt other people. I worry about that a lot in regard to my son. But I have come to understand that my differences are just that: differences. I cannot say one is good or one is bad. For example, this book has talked about the slow processing of language which certainly hinders me when I am trying to join in conversation, my understanding of how slowly language can be understood really helped my son when he was small and could not understand words quickly either. People talk about the "terrible twos" – a time when small children are likely to have a lot of tantrums, many of which are rooted in not being understood or not understanding – for the most part, my son dodged the terrible twos because I was able to go at his pace. The focus my brain is capable of makes me boring to talk to sometimes, as I just want to talk about the things my brain is focused on. But if you are interested in those things, I am brilliant not boring. The differences themselves are not what cause the hurt and harm. The hurt and harm are caused by the differences between us not being understood.

My Mummy has lots of ideas. Her brain is good at thinking

My Mummy has lots of ideas Her brain
is good at thinking

Autistic brains are good at cross-referencing information, which makes them good at coming up with ideas. An example I love is that of the paper clip challenge in which people are given a minute to think of as many things as they can that they could do with a paper clip. Neurotypical people tend to come up with a handful of ideas and autistic people come up with loads. However, the same cross-referencing makes us slow at choosing margarine in the supermarket – I just do not know which is "the right" margarine to buy.

For everyone, understanding your own brain and what it is good at and not so good at will help you to use it to be brilliant. Understanding how other people's brains work will help you not to be hurt, or to hurt others, and can enable you to use the brilliance of other people's brains alongside your own. We have all these fabulous different brains, if we get together we can use them to do fabulous different things!

I love my Mummy

Knowledge is power. Understanding is kind. Ignorance is cruel.

Aim to understand and accept your own mind. Learn its weaknesses and its strengths.

Aim to understand the minds of others too, their weaknesses and strengths.

Accept and celebrate them all for the dazzling array of beautifully different abilities that they have.

How dull the world would be if all our brains were the same.

We do not need to get rid of our differences, we need to get rid of our ignorance.

I hope my son's words will help you to build an understanding of difference.

T - #0046 - 280125 - C56 - 210/297/3 - PB - 9780367460235 - Gloss Lamination